PIANO
VOCAL
GUITAR

POPULAR CHRISTMAS SHEET MUSIC 1940-1979

T0084211

ISBN 978-1-5400-5537-8

HAL•LEONARD®

Visit Hal Leonard Online at
www.halleonard.com

Contact us:
Hal Leonard
7777 West Bluemound Road
Milwaukee, WI 53213
Email: info@halleonard.com

In Europe, contact:
Hal Leonard Europe Limited
42 Wigmore Street
Marylebone, London, W1U 2RN
Email: info@halleonardeurope.com

In Australia, contact:
Hal Leonard Australia Pty. Ltd.
4 Lentara Court
Cheltenham, Victoria, 3192 Australia
Email: info@halleonard.com.au

ALL I WANT FOR CHRISTMAS IS MY TWO FRONT TEETH

Words and Music by
DON GARDNER

CHRISTMAS IS

Lyrics by SPENCE MAXWELL
Music by PERCY FAITH

Christ-mas is sleigh - bells, Christ-mas is shar - ing,

Christ-mas is hol - ly, Christ-mas is car - ing.

BABY, IT'S COLD OUTSIDE

from the Motion Picture NEPTUNE'S DAUGHTER

By FRANK LOESSER

BLUE CHRISTMAS

Words and Music by BILLY HAYES
and JAY JOHNSON

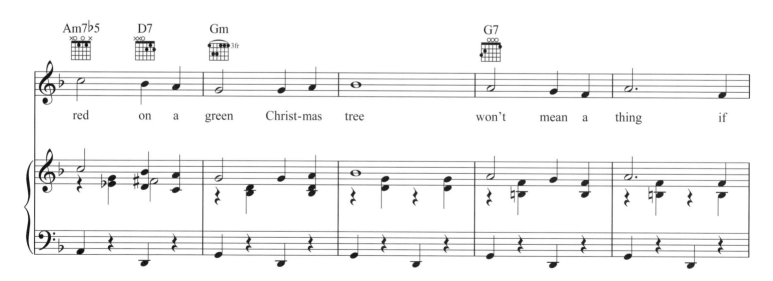

CAROLING, CAROLING

Words by WIHLA HUTSON
Music by ALFRED BURT

THE CHIPMUNK SONG

Words and Music by
ROSS BAGDASARIAN

THE CHRISTMAS SONG
(Chestnuts Roasting on an Open Fire)

Music and Lyric by MEL TORMÉ
and ROBERT WELLS

CHRISTMAS IS A-COMIN'
(May God Bless You)

Words and Music by
FRANK LUTHER

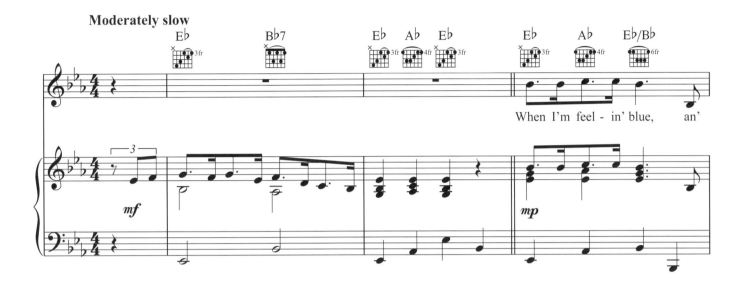

Moderately slow

When I'm feel - in' blue, an'

when I'm feel - in' low, then I start to think a-bout the hap - pi - est man I know; he

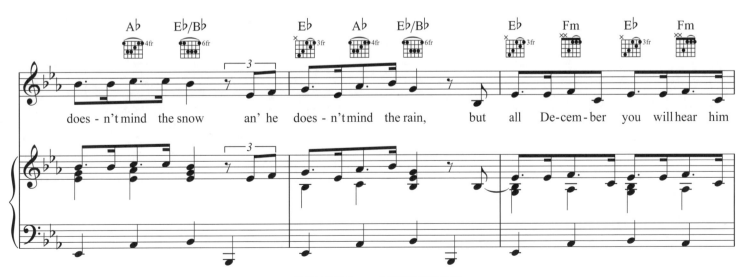

does - n't mind the snow an' he does - n't mind the rain, but all De - cem - ber you will hear him

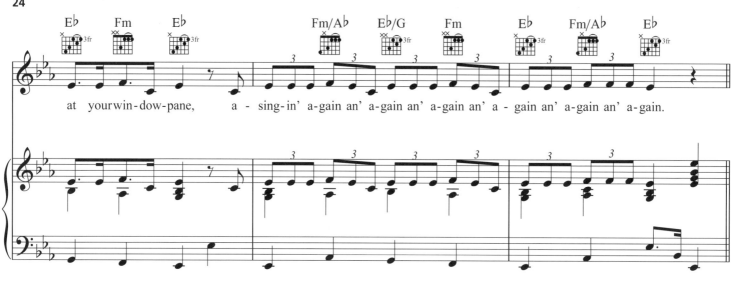

at your win-dow-pane, a - sing-in' a-gain an' a-gain an' a-gain an' a - gain an' a-gain an' a-gain.

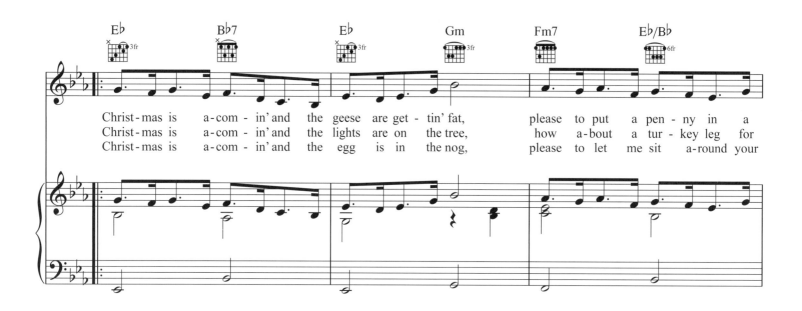

Christ-mas is a-com - in' and the geese are get - tin' fat, please to put a pen - ny in a
Christ-mas is a-com - in' and the lights are on the tree, how a-bout a tur - key leg for
Christ-mas is a-com - in' and the egg is in the nog, please to let me sit a-round your

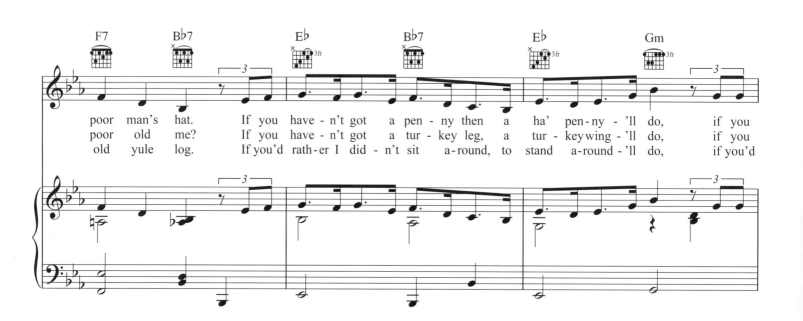

poor man's hat. If you have - n't got a pen - ny then a ha' pen-ny - 'll do, if you
poor old me? If you have - n't got a tur-key leg, a tur - key wing - 'll do, if you
old yule log. If you'd rath - er I did - n't sit a-round, to stand a-round - 'll do, if you'd

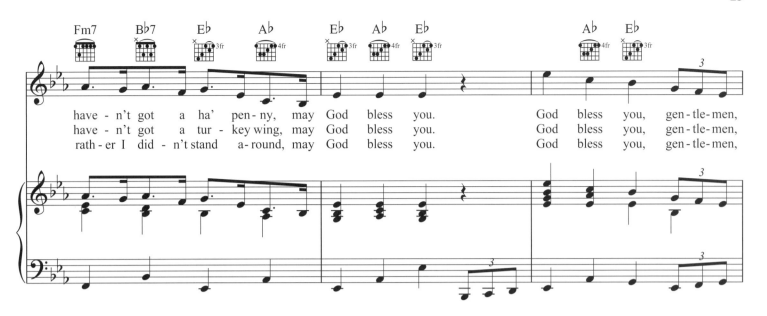

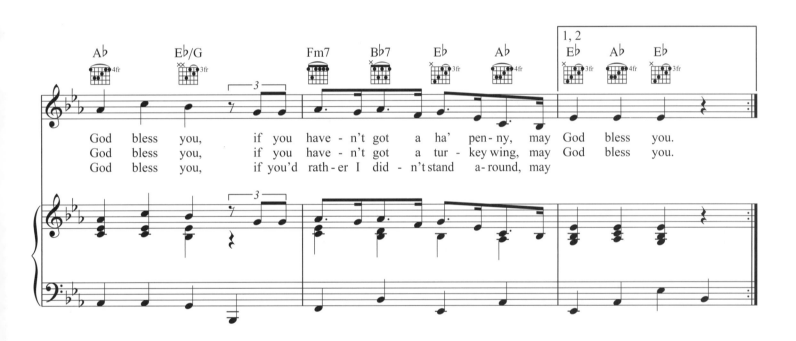

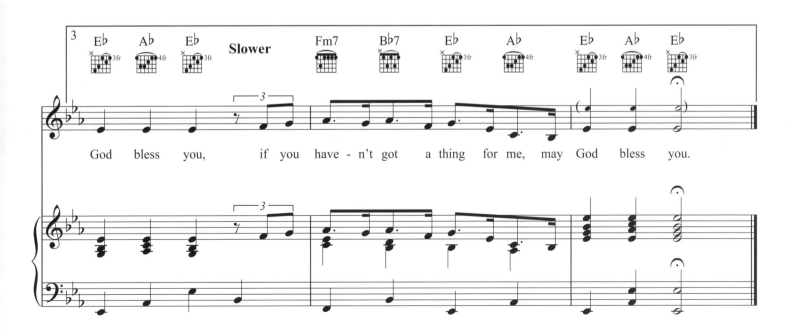

THE CHRISTMAS WALTZ

Words by SAMMY CAHN
Music by JULE STYNE

Frost-ed win-dow-panes, can-dles gleam-ing in-side, paint-ed can-dy canes on the tree; San-ta's on his way, he's filled his

CHRISTMAS TIME IS HERE

from A CHARLIE BROWN CHRISTMAS

Words by LEE MENDELSON
Music by VINCE GUARALDI

FROSTY THE SNOW MAN

Words and Music by STEVE NELSON
and JACK ROLLINS

HAPPY HOLIDAY

from the Motion Picture Irving Berlin's HOLIDAY INN

Words and Music by
IRVING BERLIN

HARD CANDY CHRISTMAS

from THE BEST LITTLE WHOREHOUSE IN TEXAS

Words and Music by
CAROL HALL

HAVE YOURSELF A MERRY LITTLE CHRISTMAS

from MEET ME IN ST. LOUIS

Words and Music by HUGH MARTIN
and RALPH BLANE

HERE COMES SANTA CLAUS
(Right Down Santa Claus Lane)

Words and Music by GENE AUTRY
and OAKLEY HALDEMAN

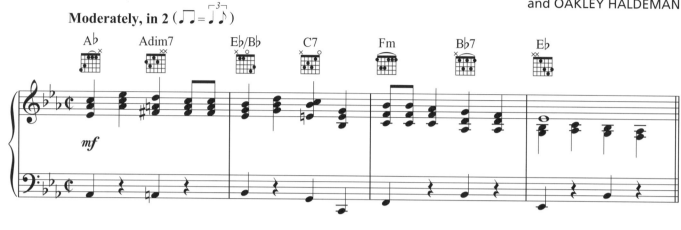

Here comes San - ta Claus! Here comes San - ta Claus! Right down San - ta Claus Lane!

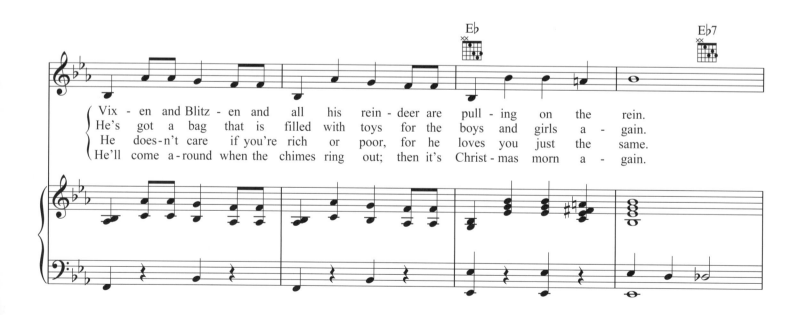

Vix - en and Blitz - en and all his rein - deer are pull - ing on the rein.
He's got a bag that is filled with toys for the boys and girls a - gain.
He does - n't care if you're rich or poor, for he loves you just the same.
He'll come a - round when the chimes ring out; then it's Christ - mas morn a - gain.

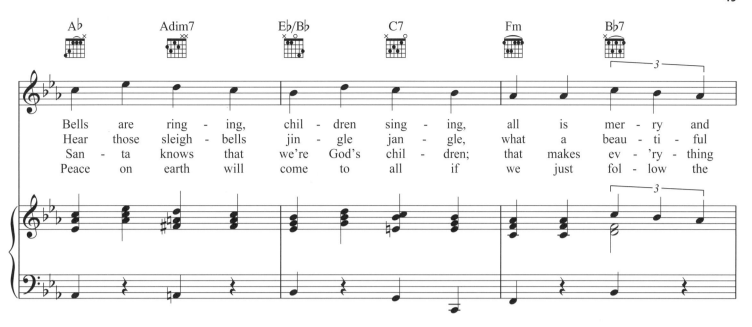

Bells are ring - ing, chil - dren sing - ing, all is mer - ry and
Hear those sleigh - bells jin - gle jan - gle, what a beau - ti - ful
San - ta knows that we're God's chil - dren; that makes ev - 'ry - thing
Peace on earth will come to all if we just fol - low the

bright.
sight.   Hang your stock - ings and say your pray'rs,
right.   Jump in bed, cov - er up your head,
light.   Fill your hearts with a Christ - mas cheer, } 'cause
    Let's give thanks to the Lord a - bove,

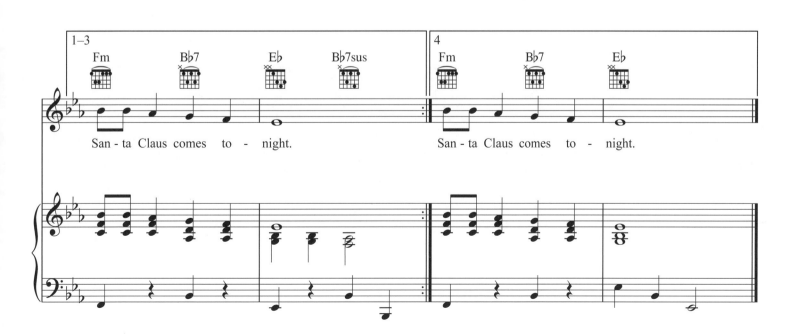

San - ta Claus comes to - night.   San - ta Claus comes to - night.

(There's No Place Like)
HOME FOR THE HOLIDAYS

Words and Music by AL STILLMAN
and ROBERT ALLEN

Moderately, with feeling

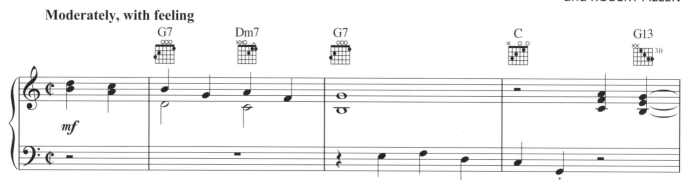

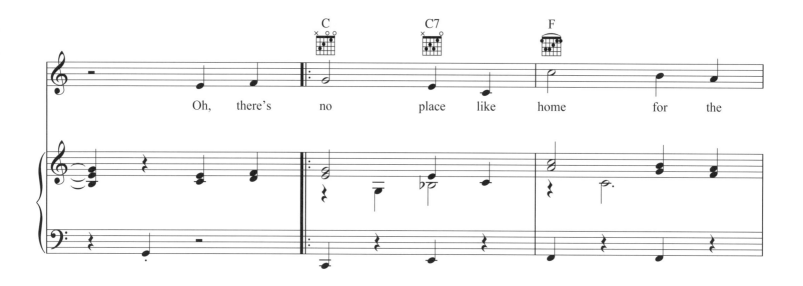

Oh, there's no place like home for the

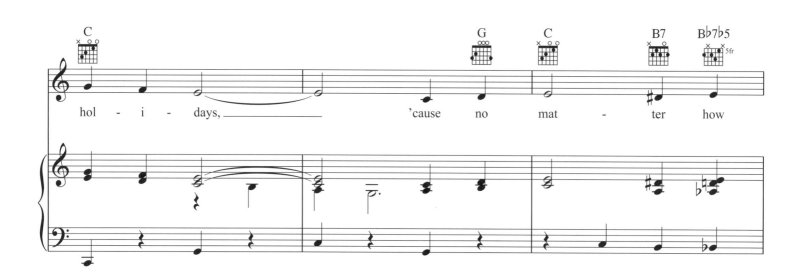

hol-i-days, _____ 'cause no mat-ter how

54

I SAW MOMMY KISSING SANTA CLAUS

Words and Music by
TOMMIE CONNOR

I HEARD THE BELLS ON CHRISTMAS DAY

Words by HENRY WADSWORTH LONGFELLOW
Adapted by JOHNNY MARKS
Music by JOHNNY MARKS

I'LL BE HOME ON CHRISTMAS DAY

Words and Music by
MICHAEL JARRETT

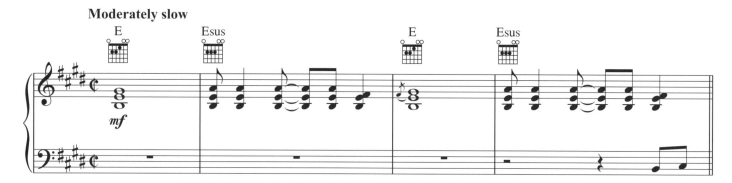

From the hills _____ of Geor - gia,
It's been so man - y times be - fore _____
There were times I'd think a - bout __ her,

a - cross the plains _____ of Ten - nes - see, __
she left that can - dle burn - ing.
all the love I _____ left be - hind.

IT'S BEGINNING TO LOOK LIKE CHRISTMAS

By MEREDITH WILLSON

It's be - gin - ning to look a lot like

Christ - mas, ev - 'ry - where you go; { Take a / There's a

look in the five and ten,   glis - ten - ing once a - gain,   with
tree in the grand ho - tel,   one in the park as well,   with the

A MARSHMALLOW WORLD

Words by CARL SIGMAN
Music by PETER DE ROSE

69

LITTLE SAINT NICK

Words and Music by BRIAN WILSON
and MIKE LOVE

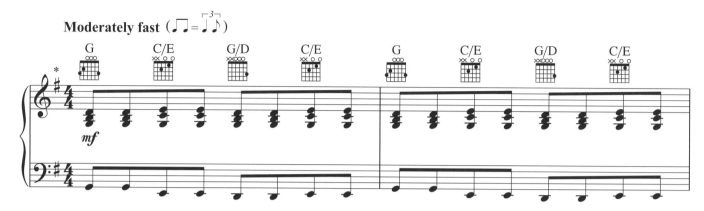

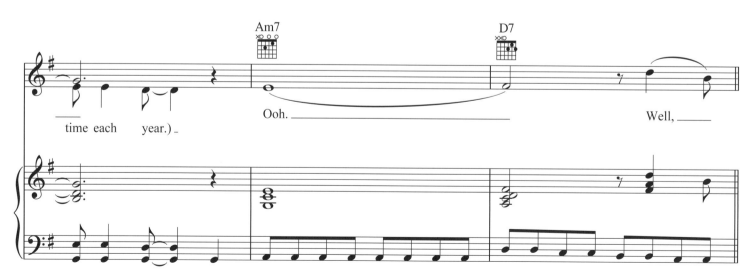

* *Recorded a half step lower.*

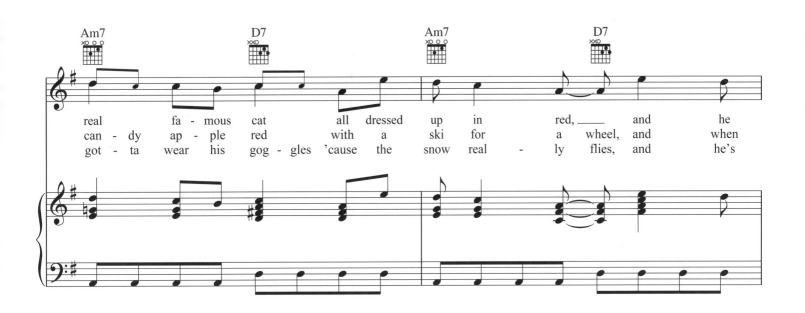

MARY'S LITTLE BOY CHILD

Words and Music by
JESTER HAIRSTON

MERRY CHRISTMAS, DARLING

Words and Music by RICHARD CARPENTER
and FRANK POOLER

Greet-ing cards have all been sent, the Christ-mas rush is through, but I still have one wish to make, a spe-cial one for you:

Mer-ry Christ-mas, dar-ling. We're a-part, that's true; but

MISTLETOE AND HOLLY

Words and Music by FRANK SINATRA,
DOK STANFORD and HENRY W. SANICOLA

Medium Bounce

Oh, by gosh, by gol - ly, it's time for mis - tle - toe and
Oh, by gosh, by jin - gle, it's time for car - ols and Kris
Oh, by gosh, by gol - ly, it's time for mis - tle - toe and

hol - ly, _____ tast - y pheas - ants, Christ - mas pres - ents,
Krin - gle, _____ o - ver - eat - ing, mer - ry greet - ings,
hol - ly, _____ fan - cy ties an' gran - ny's pies an'

To Coda ⊕

1.
coun - try-sides cov - ered with snow.

2.
from ___ rel - a - tives you don't know.

THE MOST WONDERFUL TIME OF THE YEAR

Words and Music by EDDIE POLA
and GEORGE WYLE

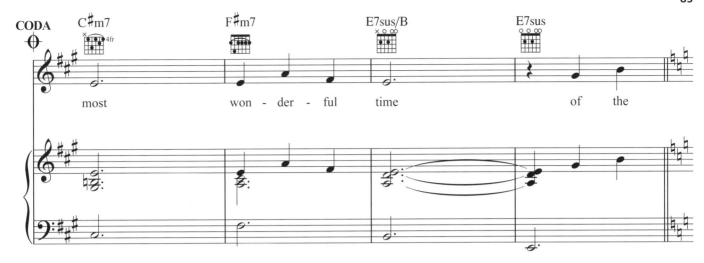

most   won - der - ful time   of the

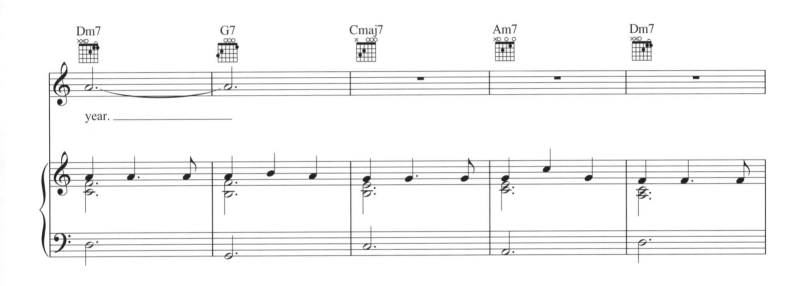

year. _____

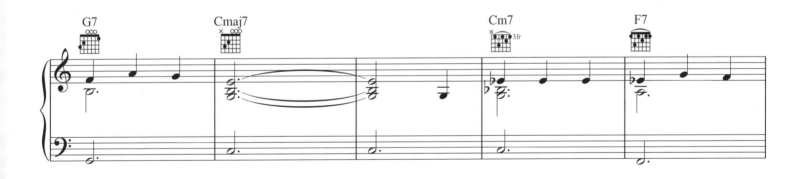

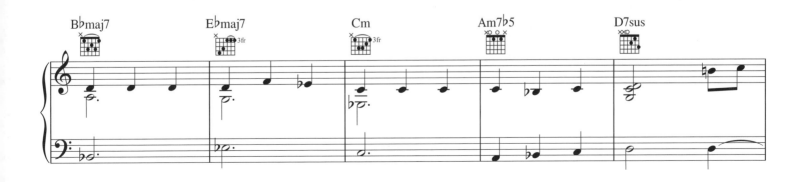

It's the most won-der-ful time of the

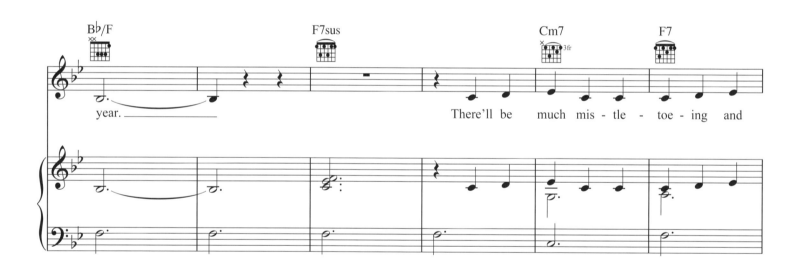

year. ___ There'll be much mis-tle-toe-ing and

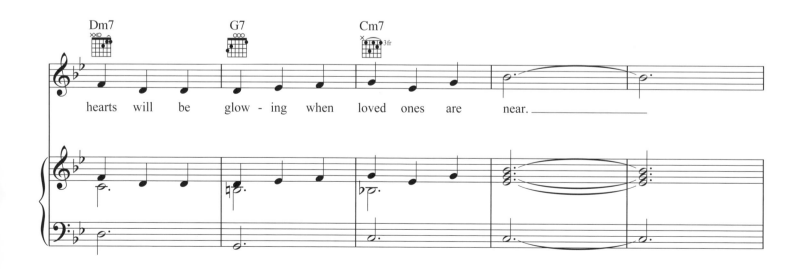

hearts will be glow-ing when loved ones are near. ___

RUDOLPH THE RED-NOSED REINDEER

Music and Lyrics by
JOHNNY MARKS

SANTA BABY

By JOAN JAVITS,
PHIL SPRINGER and TONY SPRINGER

Mis - ter "Claus," I feel as though I know ya, ____ so you won't mind if I should get fa - mil - ya, will ya?

San - ta Ba - by, just slip a sa - ble un - der the tree ___
San - ta Ba - by, one lit - tle thing I real - ly do need; ___

SANTA, BRING MY BABY BACK
(To Me)

Words and Music by CLAUDE DeMETRUIS
and AARON SCHROEDER

MISTER SANTA

Words and Music by
PAT BALLARD

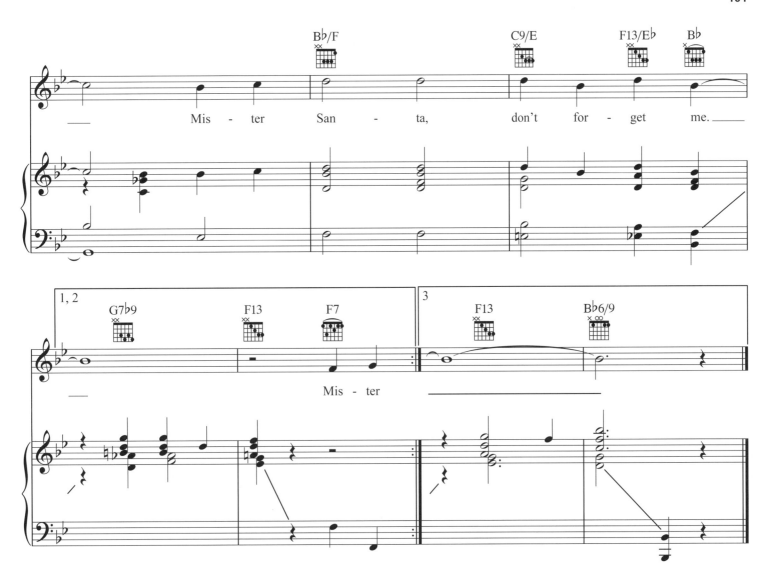

Additional Lyrics

2. Mister Santa, dear old Saint Nick,
   Be awful careful and please don't get sick.
   Put on your coat when breezes are blowin',
   And when you cross the street look where you're goin'.
   Santa, we (I) love you so,
   We (I) hope you never get lost in the snow.
   Take your time when you unpack,
   Mister Santa, don't hurry back.

3. Mister Santa, we've been so good;
   We've washed the dishes and done what we should.
   Made up the beds and scrubbed up our toesies,
   We've used a kleenex when we've blown our nosesies.
   Santa, look at our ears, they're clean as whistles,
   We're sharper than shears.
   Now we've put you on the spot,
   Mister Santa, bring us a lot.

SHAKE ME I RATTLE
(Squeeze Me I Cry)

Words and Music by HAL HACKADY
and CHARLES NAYLOR

SNOWFALL

Lyrics by RUTH THORNHILL
Music by CLAUDE THORNHILL

SILVER BELLS

from the Paramount Picture THE LEMON DROP KID

Words and Music by JAY LIVINGSTON
and RAY EVANS

SLEIGH RIDE

Music by LEROY ANDERSON
Words by MITCHELL PARISH

THE STAR CAROL

Lyric by WIHLA HUTSON
Music by ALFRED BURT

THAT CHRISTMAS FEELING

Words and Music by BENNIE BENJAMIN
and GEORGE DAVID WEISS

THIS CHRISTMAS

Words and Music by DONNY HATHAWAY
and NADINE McKINNOR

(1.,4.) Hang all the mis - tle - toe. ___ I'm gon - na get to know you bet - ter ___
(2.) Pres - ents and cards are here. ___ My world is filled with cheer and you, ___
(3.) *Piano solo ad lib.*

WHAT ARE YOU DOING NEW YEAR'S EVE?

By FRANK LOESSER

YOU'RE ALL I WANT FOR CHRISTMAS

Words and Music by GLEN MOORE
and SEGER ELLIS

WHITE CHRISTMAS
from the Motion Picture Irving Berlin's HOLIDAY INN

Words and Music by
IRVING BERLIN

CHRISTMAS COLLECTIONS
FROM HAL LEONARD
ALL BOOKS ARRANGED FOR PIANO, VOICE & GUITAR

The Best Christmas Songs Ever – 6th Edition
69 all-time favorites are included in the 6th edition of this collection of Christmas tunes. Includes: Auld Lang Syne • Coventry Carol • Frosty the Snow Man • Happy Holiday • It Came Upon the Midnight Clear • O Holy Night • Rudolph the Red-Nosed Reindeer • Silver Bells • What Child Is This? • and many more.
00359130..$27.50

The Big Book of Christmas Songs – 2nd Edition
An outstanding collection of over 120 all-time Christmas favorites and hard-to-find classics. Features: Angels We Have Heard on High • As Each Happy Christmas • Auld Lang Syne • The Boar's Head Carol • Christ Was Born on Christmas Day • Bring a Torch Jeannette, Isabella • Carol of the Bells • Coventry Carol • Deck the Halls • The First Noel • The Friendly Beasts • God Rest Ye Merry Gentlemen • I Heard the Bells on Christmas Day • It Came Upon a Midnight Clear • Jesu, Joy of Man's Desiring • Joy to the World • Masters in This Hall • O Holy Night • The Story of the Shepherd • 'Twas the Night Before Christmas • What Child Is This? • and many more. Includes guitar chord frames.
00311520..$19.95

Christmas Songs – Budget Books
Save some money this Christmas with this fabulous budget-priced collection of 100 holiday favorites: All I Want for Christmas Is You • Christmas Time Is Here • Feliz Navidad • Grandma Got Run Over by a Reindeer • Happy Holiday • I'll Be Home for Christmas • Jesus Born on This Day • Last Christmas • Merry Christmas, Baby • O Holy Night • Please Come Home for Christmas • Rockin' Around the Christmas Tree • Some Children See Him • We Need a Little Christmas • What Child Is This? • and more.
00310887..$14.99

The Definitive Christmas Collection – 3rd Edition
Revised with even more Christmas classics, this must-have 3rd edition contains 127 top songs, such as: Blue Christmas • Christmas Time Is Here • Do You Hear What I Hear • The First Noel • A Holly Jolly Christmas • Jingle-Bell Rock • Little Saint Nick • Merry Christmas, Darling • O Holy Night • Rudolph, the Red-Nosed Reindeer • Silver and Gold • We Need a Little Christmas • You're All I Want for Christmas • and more!
00311602..$24.95

The Most Requested Christmas Songs
This giant collection features nearly 70 holiday classics, from traditional carols to modern Christmas hits: Blue Christmas • Christmas Time Is Here • Deck the Hall • Feliz Navidad • I'll Be Home for Christmas • Jingle Bells • Little Saint Nick • Nuttin' for Christmas • Rudolph the Red-Nosed Reindeer • Silent Night • and more.
00001563..$19.99

The Muppet Christmas Carol
Matching folio to the blockbuster movie featuring 11 Muppet carols and eight pages of color photos. Bless Us All • Chairman of the Board • Christmas Scat • Finale - When Love Is Found/It Feels like Christmas • It Feels like Christmas • Marley and Marley • One More Sleep 'Til Christmas • Room in Your Heart • Scrooge • Thankful Heart • When Love Is Gone.
00312483..$16.99

Tim Burton's The Nightmare Before Christmas
This book features 11 songs from Tim Burton's creepy animated classic, with music and lyrics by Danny Elfman. Songs include: Jack's Lament • Jack's Obsession • Kidnap the Sandy Claws • Making Christmas • Oogie Boogie's Song • Poor Jack • Sally's Song • This Is Halloween • Town Meeting Song • What's This? • Finale/Reprise.
00312488..$16.99

A Sentimental Christmas Book
An outstanding collection of nearly 30 beloved Christmas favorites, including: All I Want for Christmas Is You • Blue Christmas • Christmas Lights • The Christmas Shoes • The Christmas Song (Chestnuts Roasting on an Open Fire) • Christmas Time Is Here • Christmases When You Were Mine • Fairytale of New York • Grown-Up Christmas List • Have Yourself a Merry Little Christmas • (There's No Place Like) Home for the Holidays • I'll Be Home for Christmas • Please Come Home for Christmas • Silver Bells • Somewhere in My Memory • Where Are You Christmas? • White Christmas • You're All I Want for Christmas • and more.
00236830..$14.99

Ultimate Christmas – 3rd Edition
100 seasonal favorites: Auld Lang Syne • Bring a Torch, Jeannette, Isabella • Carol of the Bells • The Chipmunk Song • Christmas Time Is Here • The First Noel • Frosty the Snow Man • Gesù Bambino • Happy Holiday • Happy Xmas (War Is Over) • Hymne • Jesu, Joy of Man's Desiring • Jingle-Bell Rock • March of the Toys • My Favorite Things • The Night Before Christmas Song • Pretty Paper • Silver and Gold • Silver Bells • Suzy Snowflake • What Child Is This • The Wonderful World of Christmas • and more.
00361399..$22.99